# They Came So Naturally

Janice P. Wright

Kingdom Builders Publications LLC

© 2018 Janice P. Wright

SECOND EDITION

Kingdom Builders Publications, LLC

All rights reserved. No part of this book may be reproduced or transmitted in any form or by any means without written permission from the author.

Printed in the USA

ISBN: 978-0-692-92870-7

Library of Congress Control Number: 2017950600

**Authored by**
Janice P Wright

**Editor**
Dr. Gene E Gary-Williams
Kingdom Builders Publications Editorial Staff

**Photographer**
Shantia Wheeler – TAYke My Pic Photography

Cover Design
LoMar Designs

Scripture quotations marked KJV are taken for the HOLY BIBLE KING JAMES VERSION Scripture quotations marked NIV are taken from the HOLY BIBLE NEW INTERNATIONAL BIBLE VERSION
www.biblegateway.com

## This Book Belongs to

Janice P. Wright

Lord, I ask that you give everyone who reads this book of poetry, a Holy Ghost Hug! In Jesus name I pray. Amen
Be Blessed 4 U R A Blessing ☺

# DEDICATION

Dedicated in love to my granddaughter,
Areyanne Diamond Prather

Janice P. Wright

# CONTENTS

| | |
|---|---|
| DEDICATION | v |
| INTRODUCTION | 1 |
| WHAT COLOR IS YOUR ROSE | 6 |
| 4 MY SISTERS | 8 |
|     SPEAK IT | 9 |
|     SPEAK TO ME | 10 |
|     BEAUTY | 11 |
|     THE SHUNAMITE WOMAN | 12 |
|     MRS. JOB | 14 |
|     THIS IS A LOVE STORY | 18 |
|     MY THOUGHTS ON GOOD FRIDAY | 21 |
|     JUST FOR YOU | 24 |
|     WHO WILL GO | 26 |
|     THIS IS OUR QUEST | 28 |
| 4 MY PEEPS | 30 |
|     WE ARE BECAUSE THEY WERE | 31 |
|     SIS' GRANDS | 33 |
|     MR. FRANK | 36 |
|     QUEEN OF OUR TRIBE | 38 |
|     I NEVER WROTE A POEM FOR MY DAD | 40 |
|     FUNNY VALENTINE | 43 |
|     FEELIN IT | 46 |

| | |
|---|---|
| HOW CAN I SING IN A STRANGE LAND? | 47 |
| OVERCOME | 49 |
| LET HE WHO IS WITHOUT, CAST THE FIRST STONE | 51 |
| WE CAME… WE SAW… WE CONQUERED! | 52 |
| 4 THE LOVE OF U | 54 |
| I HEAR TALES | 55 |
| MY GENESIS | 57 |
| IN TOUCH | 59 |
| THA' MY POEM | 61 |
| ME & NIKKI G | 62 |
| MY MAN | 64 |
| SOMETIMES | 66 |
| DEAF-CEPTION | 67 |
| THEY CAME SO NATURALLY | 68 |
| GRINDIN IN THE NAME OF THE LORD | 70 |
| MORE ABOUT THE AUTHOR | 74 |

## INTRODUCTION

I have been told that everything we go through happens for a reason. I heard it said that God won't put more on us that we can bear and that the things which we go through are not for ourselves but to help someone else. Even our pain and suffering is for the benefit of others. My story sadly enough is one among many African American mothers, yet, it is unique to me. In 1977, I was blessed with my first man-child. I prepared his room and his basset with Winnie the Pooh coordinating bedding. I purchased him a sweater set. You know the ones, with the caps and the little booties. I was excited about his homecoming. I loved him dearly.

In 2005, I lost my son to the violence and the senseless killing on the streets of Prince George's County. It was all over the evening news, there were write ups about it in the Washington Post newspaper, the Prince George Garzett, it was even on the internet! An article that went something like this; "An Upper Marlboro man was shot and killed last night about 8:40. Anthony Demond Prather, 28 years old of the 1200 block of Old Colony Drive was found dead on the scene. Police said that Prather had been standing outside the home when at least one person approached him and shot him multiple times. A motive was not determined."

Have you ever read your bible and scripture just popped up from the page and pierce your soul? I wasn't able to read those articles during that particular time. But, what I could decipher through my tears, pierced my heart. My son, my boy, had been killed and "a motive has not been determined!"

Well, just like in the beginning when I prepared for his homecoming, I had to prepare for his homegoing. This time instead of a basset, I purchased a casket. I had to pick out his clothes and the funeral home instructed me to purchase him a cap. Why? Because he had been shot in the head. Not only did I lose my boy, but I nearly lost my mind. I could not believe that this was happening to me. You see, "oh death where is your string?" had stung me more than enough times, I thought. In 2000, I lost my grandfather, 2002, I lost my father, 2003 I lost my mother, and this was only 2005. Oh God, not my boy!

So, the following Mother's Day, I wrote myself a Mother's Day poem titled, "What Color is Your Rose?" When I was growing up, we were given roses to wear on Mother's Day in honor of our mother. The roses had special meanings. If you wore a white rose; it meant that your mother was dead, a yellow rose was in memory of your mother and the pink and red roses symbolized that your mother was alive. Red was my son's favorite color, so at his funeral I wore red and brought a bed spread of red roses for his casket. A red rose also means I love you.

There were three things that helped me to get over the death of my son. One of them was the Word of God. I quoted scriptures that had been embedded in my soul. Scriptures like, Psalms 30: verse 5, "Weeping may endure for a night but joy cometh in the morning." Even though, I did not have the energy to lift my head off my tear stained pillow, to get out of bed, let alone leave my home. I kept saying, "Joy Cometh." I knew that I was in a storm and that I was battling for my life. I was confused, disturbed, angry and hurt. I was drowning in the sea of life. But God! God spoke to my storm and said, "Peace be still" I told myself, be still and know that He is God. Know that he knows all about it, that he knows who did this awful thing, even if the police did not. God knows and He knows just how much it hurts and exactly what I was going through. God said that vengeance belongs to him. "Peace be still." I reminded myself that the just shall "LIVE" by faith, not die. It was by faith in God that I made it through.

The second thing that helped me to go through was being able to go before the Lord and just let go. At my church, Life Source International Church, in Baltimore, Maryland, we have an open door policy or should I say an open alter policy. I would make my ways to that alter and kneel before God, crying my heart out. I would cry like Hannah cried for a son. You know that cry, that deep in your gut cry, the cry that when you open your mouth and not a sound come out, tears won't fall from your eyes. The Word of God said, "Blessed are they that mourn, for they shall be comforted." God comforted me.

The third thing was that God had encamped angels all around me, angels in the spirit and angels in the flesh. One of those angels was my sister Geneva. She was on the scene the night that my son was killed. She knew that I needed someone to be with me, so she called my cousin Robyn. Robyn left her home in Virginia and traveled to Baltimore to minister to me. She sat with me, prayed with me, and cried with me. She was a sweet gentle spirit that helped to strengthen me. My Aunt Betty came from South Carolina, I call her my big sister, she protected me and gave me guidance. I thank God for my earthly angels.

My family was falling apart. My husband had lost a son, my son had lost his brother, my sisters and brothers had lost their nephew and my nieces and nephews had lost their cousin. We are a close knitted family, there was so much grief. My five-year-old granddaughter, Arey had lost her father. My Arey is another angel in my life. She inherited her father's smile and this brings me joy!

*But Jesus said, Suffer little children, and forbid them not, to come unto me: for of such is the kingdom of heaven.* **Matthew 19:14 King James Version (KJV)**

I have a great nephew, Aaron who during that time would call me, "Yana." His mother would try to correct him and tell him that my name was Aunt Janice. He would reply, "No, she Yana." I told her to let the baby call me what he wanted. Yet, I was curious as why this child had taken it upon himself to call me "Yana." So, I googled the word "YANA" I found out that definition for "Yana" meant, "one on a spiritual journey!" Then I dug a little deeper and was astound to discover that the acronyms for Y.A.N.A. stood for "You Are Never Alone." Out of the mouths of babes, I am Yana!

I say to you, this world in not our home. We are all here on a spiritual journey. God said that, he will never leave you nor forsake you. No matter what you are going through, "YANA," you are never alone. Amen.

# THEY CAME SO NATURALLY

*This poem is dedicated to all the Mothers, who lost their loved ones to the senseless killings on the streets. One of your flowers is missing from your garden this Mother's Day. I just want you to know that I thought of him, so I am praying for you.*

Janice P. Wright

# WHAT COLOR IS YOUR ROSE
### A Mother's Day Poem to Myself

What Color is Your Rose?
Is it yellow, white, pink, or red?
Is it yellow like the fading memories of my loved one's voice?
Or is it white?
White like the satin sheet that lined my loved one's coffin bed?
Or is it pink?
Pink like the whites of my eyes
from crying over my love one's grave
My rose, my rose is Red,
Red, like the blood on the blood-stained streets,
where my baby laid dead.
Didn't they know or even care, that someone, somewhere,
loved that somebody, who they hated, enough to murder?
By the way, Happy Mother's Day!

# THEY CAME SO NATURALLY

# 4 MY SISTERS

*Some of the poems in this book were written in a matter to help young sisters take a look at biblical characters from a different aspect. Some are poetic, some are thought provoking, others are humorous. They were written to let us know that nothing is new under the sun, even though the world tries to tell us differently. The modern day world has tried to classified our behaviors, thereby, attempting to justify our actions. I believe that the almighty God gave us these stories to help us along the way and to give us understanding, guidance and deliverance.*

## SPEAK IT

*⁹ With the tongue we praise our Lord and Father, and with it we curse human beings, who have been made in God's likeness. ¹⁰ Out of the same mouth come praise and cursing. My brothers and sisters, this should not be.* **James 3:9 KJV**

# We should use our tongues to:

# Speak Blessing

# Speak healing

# Speak Life

# Speak Love

# Speak Peace

Janice P. Wright

# Speak to Me

Oh Father, the Giver of Life
Bless me this day with love,
peace, and harmony
Speak Life to my soul
Oh Lord, speak Life to me
In the mid-day
Touch me from heaven above
Touch me with your finger of love and
I will in turn touch others by sharing,
giving, and caring
Speak Love to my soul
Oh Lord, speak Love to me
The sun may not shine all day
Some dark clouds may come my way
Protect me from the things I cannot see
Speak Peace to my soul
Oh My Lord, Speak Peace to me
When the midnight comes, my body is weary
and my strength is almost gone,
If I never see another dawn
Speak Rest to my soul,
Oh Lord, Speak Rest unto me

# BEAUTY

*If Beauty is in the eye of the beholder*
*Then…*
*It is the eye that beholds the Beauty*
*If…*
*It is the eye that beholds the sight*
*Then…*
*It is the mind that beholds the insight*
*If…*
*It is the mind that beholds the insight*
*Then…*
*Beauty must come from within,*
*Think about it…*

*You should be known for the beauty that comes from within, the unfading beauty of a gentle and quiet, spirit, which is so precious to God.* **1 Peter 3:4**

# THE SHUNAMITE GIRL

*I*f you have read the Song of Solomon, then you are familiar with story of the Shunamite girl and all of her glory. The bible states that she was dark, yet comely. Comely, meaning, beautiful, charming, and full of grace, for the love of God shone upon her face.

She dwelled in Shunem with her mother and her brothers. She would neglect her own vineyards, just to attend to the vineyards of others.

Solomon was the son of King David. He was tall, dark, handsome, and wise. He had many concubines and wives, yet the Shunamite girl was the apple of his eyes. He said that she was like a Lilly amongst thorn, for the others talked about her as sure as you are born.

Can you imagine their mockery, "My beloved this, my beloved that, what makes her beloved so much better than any other?"

"If you ask me, Solomon should have chosen another."

"Most beautiful of all women, huh, that's a matter of opinion."

The Shunamite girl paid them no mind, she wore Solomon's shield upon her heart. Yes, she was guilty, for in her own words, she did state that "My beloved is mine and I am his," and so she gave him all she had to give.

Arise! My young sisters, Arise! For you are the apples of God's eyes. You are his Rose of Sharon, his Lilies of the Valley. You may not have riches, fortune, or fame but God knows each of you by name.

Place his shield upon your hearts. Give him all you have to give. He deserves your love for as long as you live.

Arise! My young sister, Arise! For just like the Shunamite girl, you have been appointed to be queens! You have been chosen by the King of kings! Amen.

Janice P. Wright

# Mrs. Job

*[7] So Satan went out from the presence of the LORD and afflicted Job with painful sores from the soles of his feet to the crown of his head. [8] Then Job took a piece of broken pottery and scraped himself with it as he sat among the ashes. [9] His wife said to him, "Are you still maintaining your integrity? Curse God and die!"*
*Job 2:7-9 NIV*

Okay, let's get the story straight, everyone knows that Job was a righteous man. Right? He lost everything he had and he didn't even put up a fight.

Instead… in great anguish, he ripped off all his clothes and shaved his head. Then he did something really strange, he got down on his knees and worshipped the Lord.

"Naked into the world I came and naked I'll go out," he did not scream, ask why, nor did he shout, "The Lord gave and the Lord has taken away, blessed be the name of the Lord,"
What a wonderful, virtuous thing for Job to say!

Behind every great man, there is a great woman, so the saying goes. I believe this is true, even of the wife of Job.
What was her name, anyway? The Bible did not say
We don't know . . . so out of respect, let just call her Mrs. Job.
Not that I am taking sides but let's look at this story through her eyes.
I am just saying. If Job was a rich man, then as his wife, she was a rich woman. If he had servants, then so did she.

She borne his children and she loved them too
Not only did he lose everything, but she did too
For richer, for poorer, in sickness and in health
Mr. & <u>Mrs. Job</u> lost their children, social status, and wealth.

Now, Job was permitted to express himself before the Lord, In a moment of weakness, I believe, he even cursed the day, he was conceived. What were her thoughts, when the servants came to tell of Job great fall? She was his wife and the mother of his children after all.

Oh, Mrs. Job, who came and comforted you when you cried? What did you do, when you heard that all your children had died? How did it feel to watch your husband turn to bones, right before your eyes? Mrs. Job should not have been criticized.

After all, everything that Job went through, she was right there by his side. When his friends talked about him, she had to endure their criticism When they told him to confess that he was not a man of righteous, and that he had done something wrong. She had to wonder, how long will this go on? I am sure she had a moment, and just couldn't take it anymore. She was isolated, and sick of tired of watching her husband suffering and scratching at his sores.

That's why she told Job to curse his God and die.

She wanted him out of his misery, I am sure that's the reason why.

God is a forgiving God, surely, He understood what Mrs. Job was going through I believe it was His call, I am just saying, that's all.

Job told her that she did not sound like his wife, that she sounded like a fool, (that was kind of cruel).

What did he expect her to say or do? No, she was not the wife he knew. She was a mother mourning the loss of her babies, and wondering what had happened to their life.

She was a woman who had lost hope and one of little faith.

She was hurting. She needed comforting, not confronting.

A little mercy and some grace.

Lest we forget, what do you think, were her actions and/or reactions appropriate?

Just in case you do not know, the story ends like it began

The Lord blessed Job with more houses, more cattle, more servants and even more. He blessed him with more sons and more daughters just like before.

The Bible even mentions his daughters by name, Jeminah, Keziah and Keren, but, no mention of Mrs. Job (what a shame).
Job's daughters were the most beautiful women in all the land. I believe they resemble their mother; Mrs. Job's a beautiful woman who stood by her man.
 I am just saying, that's all!

Janice P. Wright

# This is a Love Story

*<sup>16</sup>And Laban had two daughters: the name of the elder was Leah, and the name of the younger was Rachel.<sup>17</sup> Leah was tender eyed; but Rachel was beautiful and well favoured.<sup>18</sup> And Jacob loved Rachel;* **GENESIS** *29: 16-18 KIV*

ow from the moment Jacob saw Rachel, he was attracted to her, for she was beautiful.

He asked her father Laban for her hand in marriage and her father agreed. But on his wedding night, Jacob was deceived. Jacob thought it was Rachel in his bed but her father had given him Leah instead. Because Leah was the older of the two, her father explained that this was the traditional thing to do.

Now Jacob was the master of deception. He was involved in a sibling rivalry of his own. He had stolen his brother Esau's birth rights, that was the reason he had to leave his home. Esau vowed to kill him and Jacob was afraid of his brother's fury. Rachel was beautiful but Leah was not, in fact her name meant "Weary."

Jacob had labored seven years for Rachel, the love of his life, but now, Leah was his wife. Leah wanted her husband to love her but Jacob loved her sister Rachel instead. The spirits of jealous, envy and hatred ran rapidly through their heads. Leah was jealous, Rachel was envious and Jacob hated. But remember, I told you this is a love story and love is never over rated.

Man looks on the outside but God looks at the heart. Leah yearned to be loved by her husband, but Jacob wanted no part. The Lord saw that Leah was unloved by her husband.

So, He blessed her with four sons and Rachel with none. Her first son, she named, Reuben, Leah said, "Surely the Lord has looked upon my affliction, now my husband will love me." (Yet he didn't)

With her second son, Leah proclaimed, "The Lord had heard that I was hated, that is why he gave me this son, and Simeon will be his name. Surely, now I will be loved by my husband." (Yet, she wasn't)

Her third son was named Levi – meaning attached, Leah thought her husband would love her for sure this time. She had given him three sons and her sister had given him none. (But he didn't)

It was not until the birth of her fourth son that Leah decided to give God praise, so she named him Judah, meaning "Praise." Leah thought that having babies would win her husband's love and affection, she was looking for love in all the wrong directions.

Leah borne two more sons, Issachar, which meant hired and Zebulun, meaning a good dowry. "Now my husband will dwell with me," she thought. But the truth is, real love can never be brought.

The Lord our God is as a loving God and he blessed Leah in spike of herself. Perhaps you think Leah's predicament was an unfortunate mishap. Sometimes, we humans may not understand, but God never makes a mistake, He always has a plan.

For out of Leah's wound came Israel's priestly line, the tribe of Levi. From the tribe of Judah came our Lord, the Messiah. See, I told you, this was a love story and to God be all the Glory! It is through Him that we able to cope for God loves the unloved, He is the giver of life and hope.

THEY CAME SO NATURALLY

# My Thoughts on Good Friday

*For God So Love the World That He Gave His Only Begotten Son That Whosoever Believe on Him Shall Not Perish but Have Everlasting Life*
*JOHN -3:16 KIV*

What a horrible day for the world. Oh, the tragedy! Oh, the drama! God the Father had turned his back on this world of cruel and evil people. He caused the whole earth to shake, an earth quake like no other. On that day, God took his eyes off this earth, there was darkness. Oh, how great was that darkness.

How did the people feel when they realized they were responsible for the death of Jesus the Christ? Could this have really been the Messiah? Was He really the Chosen One, the Son of God?

What about Mary, the Mother of Jesus. Jesus was the gift of life that God gave her. He was the gift that she gave to the world.

*She watched...*

As he grew, from baby Jesus, to the young man who taught the Elders. He became the preacher, the teacher, the healer, the miracle worker. He was a good son. She was so proud of him.

Oh, how she loved him. He was her beloved son also.

*She watched...*

As they bruised his body, hammered nails in his hands and in his feet, the blood streaming down his precious face. She saw the pain in his eyes like no other, the helplessness, he was helpless, and she was helpless. He seemed so powerless. There was nothing she could do to reverse this action, absolutely nothing. Only God had the power to stop them. But, God the Father had turned his back on this world of cruel and evil people. Oh, the tragedy! Oh, the drama!

*She listened...*

At the foot of the cross, she listened to his shallow breaths, his excruciating moans, and his agonizing groans.

As he prayed for them, "Father, forgive them, for they know not what they do." Why did he love this world so much, that he would sacrifice his own life? Didn't He know how much this would hurt, to see her son: CRUCIFIED, BEATEN, BATTERED, BRUISE, WOUNDED, WHIPPED, MUTILATED, and MURDERED, Didn't He know?

*She felt...*

His pain, as he hung there on that the cross, she felt his pain, she suffered his agony. She cried until she had no more tears to cry. When he died, she died, although she lived, she died...

What a horrible day for the world. Oh, the tragedy! Oh, the drama! What a catastrophe!

A WORLD WITHOUT JESUS! Think about it. No hope for the coming of the Messiah. No hope for the coming of the King. No hope for the coming of God's Son.

No hope for tomorrow,

No hope,

Hopeless…

But, after his death, Jesus had some unfinished business to finalize. He went to the pits of Hell and Satan had to get the hell out of there!

On the second day, all that day, Satan, was permitted to roam the earth. Satan was mad as hell because he knew he had been defeated! Oh, the tragedy! Oh, the drama! What a catastrophe!

But that's not how the story ends, for on the third day. . .

Joy came in the morning!

Early Sunday Morning!

Jesus Arose!

Resurrected!

FULL OF HOPE!

Hallelujah!

Amen.

Janice P. Wright

# JUST FOR YOU

It was just for you that Jesus died

Just for you that they pierced him in his sides

Yes, just for you that they hung him on a tree

For you, yes you, that he went to Calvary

For you who is filled with hatred, envy, and strife

It was for you that Jesus gave up his life

Jesus, perfect, pure, and clean without a spot

For thirty-three years, he lived and sinned not

For you, the lonely, desolate, and confused

It was you that Jesus refused

He refused to come down from the cross

Just to save you who are lost

For you, who won't believe the truth, that Jesus is Lord

and for you who ask for more proof

Here's proof, just because He loves you

Jesus suffered all that agony

Not only does He love you but

He also died to save sinners like you and me.

Thank you Lord, is all I can say

Thank you for your love and your saving grace

Save another with this poem, Father, I pray

Janice P. Wright

# WHO WILL GO

*35 For I was hungry and you fed me; I was thirsty and you gave me water; I was a stranger and you invited me into your homes; 36 naked and you clothed me; sick and in prison, and you visited me.'*
*Matthew 25:35*

These were the words he was told
There is no cure for your disease
We have done every test known to man
Go home, get your house in order,
Write your will, and make funeral plans

She sat on the bed, the tears just
streaming down her eyes
Why, Why? Why? She cried.
Life is not worth the living, all take and no giving
She had been raped, abandoned,
abused, and misused

Who will go?

To offer up words of encouragement,
and let them know?
To wipe away the tear
or just sit and silently hold

He decided to take manners in his own hand,
Now, he is in a place where a man can't be a man
In jail without any bail

The cardboard sign read H-H-H
Homeless, Hungry, HELP
Now I know what you must be thinking to yourself
But God forbid, if you were in their shoes
Would you know what to do?
See, it could have been you,
with no home, and all alone

Substance Abuse, Sexual Immorality, Idolatry,
the thief comes to steal and to kill, literally
the world is lost without a savior
and that's the reality

Who will go to let them know?

Jesus loves them still, and abundant life is His will
Who, who, who will go? To let them know
Eternal life is theirs to have and to hold,
and Jesus was crucified to save their souls,
Who will pick up the cross of compassion and let
them know that GOD SENT HIS BEST
THIS, THIS IS YOUR QUEST

Janice P. Wright

# THIS IS OUR QUEST

To bless and be a blessing

To Serve and be a Servants

We are the light in this world of darkness

We are not powerless but full of POWER

We are worry free, fearless,

standing on God's promises

The Power of God and His love empowers us

To speak things into existence,

To teach without resistance

Through God's Words, we have been given wisdom and knowledge

Through Christ Jesus, we have been given Power and authority

To bring salvation to those who believe,

 To give Hope, Peace and understanding

To all who will receive


Let those who have ears to hear, HEAR…

The word of God as it spoken through and to His anointed

Preach on Preacher, Teach on Teacher

Pray until the Power of God comes down

Until God's Glory fills the earth

Make every effort to confirm your calling

Now unto Him who is able to keep you from falling

Be the light for the world

Go, Go, one on one, or two by two, allowing God to use you

Full of POWER… The POWER of God

For this is our quest.

In the Precious Name of Jesus be Blessed. Amen

# 4 MY PEEPS

## We Are Because

# We Are Because They Were…

### Prather Family Reunion Poem

We Are Because They Were…

Slaves, Sharecroppers, Farmers, "Cotton Pickin, Colored Folks"

We are because they were…

Carpenters, Bricklayers, Mechanics, Painters, Shoemakers, Service men

They were Maids, Cooks, Seamstress, and Housewives

We are because they were…

Strong enough, Big enough, Bold enough, Powerful, and Black enough

We are the descendants of Big, Bold, Black, African American men and women, who cared enough to instill in us Biblical Principles, Family Values, and Pride

And… we are wise enough to realize that we cannot be grateful enough to the Lord our God for blessing us with our Ancestors.

Because they were…

We are!

# Embrace your Heritage!

THEY CAME SO NATURALLY

# Sis' Grands

Remember Grandma?

Remember, when we all got together, the way she would hugged us and smothered us in between her breasts, as we tried to catch our breath. We laughed!

Even though sometimes the reason we were together was no laughing matter. We laughed!

Remember the time when our Mama left Daddy. Grandma, made breakfast, lunch and dinner and sandwiches and baked cakes, peach cobblers and pies, while our mama cried. But we didn't t know no better, so we ate all that comfort food. And we laughed!

Lord, the summers, remember the summers we spent together, lemonade, watermelon, homemade ice cream and the fan. Even though she had an air conditioner, Grandma didn't like no air conditioner.

And Lawdy, it was hot in that house but, we laughed!

Remember on Saturdays, when Grandma stripped all the beds and washed the sheets and hung them on the clothes line and the hot summer wind would blow, making the sheets flap in the air and we ran between them just a laughing. Remember when we saw Grandma's bloomers hanging on the line, and how we rolled on the ground, just a laughing!

You remember, when Grandma went to the hair dresser and got her hair curled, then she came home to wash your hair, plait our little sister hair, and press mine? By the time she finished with our hair, she didn't have a curl in her haired. And we laughed!

Remember, how on Sunday mornings, grandma, ironed our dresses, hemmed the boys' pants, laid out Granddaddy's suit, rolled biscuits for breakfast, prayed for the sick and shut in, finished making dinner, and sent us to Sunday school with Granddaddy?

Phew! Then she got dress, put in her teeth, and put that red lip stick on her lips, then popped a stick of dentine gum in her mouth, came to church, sang her song, and prayed her prayer and cried aloud. And we laughed!

Do you remember the time we played in the rain and made mud puddles and foot prints in the sand? Remember how we got all dirty and when grandma came home, mud and sand was all over the house and we had taken baths and left cakes of sand in the tub? Grandma was so mad that her jaws were shaking as she fussed at us.

Remember, remember, when Grandma went across the road to get a switch from the tree and we watched afar from the screen door, as she searched for the greenest switch and then she shelved the leave off with one swift movement and we screamed so loud and cried like babies as she walked back to the house.

Remember? Remember, Granddaddy came home just in time to keep her from whipping our behinds and we were real quiet at the supper table and Grandma sent us to bed early and we listened to crickets as they made sleep sounds, and even though Grandma told us not to make a sound, underneath our pillows, we laughed!

We were one big happy family, Grandma made us think we were all sisters and brothers and we did not know any better, we were just happy to be together. Remember those times? Remember the things Grandma use to say, like, "All closed eyes ain't sleep." Remember the kisses she gave. Remember, remember how she protected us. Remember the way she loved? Remember the way people use to say, that's one of Sis' grands, and how proud it made us feel.

Remember, how it hurt, when she died? We cried. Remember?

Janice P. Wright

# MR. FRANK

On a summer August morn
Unto them a son was born
A son who was obedient, kind, and warm
When he grew into a man,
he took his sweetie by her hand
Before the preacher they would stand
And he became her husband
For his family, he did his best
Around the table they would pray
A tradition that goes on this very day
To some he was a brother
A friend indeed to others
This man was also a teacher
About that much from being a preacher
Many had come to him for advice
Not only was he kind, he was also nice

A cornerstone, a strong foundation

This man was to four generations

Honor, glory, and praise

From all those that he raised

This young man, bless his soul

Lived to be eighty-three years old

Now, he has a home in glory

And that's the beginning of Mr. Frank's story.

Janice P. Wright

# QUEEN OF OUR TRIBE

Our mother possessed a quite gentle spirit

She floated with the gracefulness of a dove

Within her spirit she exhibited God's love

She had a love for life and the simple things

Like coming together for family gathering

These things are beyond measure and compare

When we needed encouragement, she was always there

Her kisses would greet us when we meet,

It was her gentle tone that made us listen whenever she would speak

Her laughter could warm the coldest heart

And after the visit, with a kiss we would depart

Life for her was a struggle, yet as sweet as she could be

She was a woman of strength and dignity

When we were young, like an eagle she stretched out her wings to cover her love ones and she protected us from all kind of things

Queen Eartha, the Mother of Our Tribe

It's because of her that we are alive

Children, grandchildren, and great-grands

Stand and clap your hands as we honor and remember,

Our Mom, Nanny, one in the same

Queen Eartha Mae, bless her name

Thank you God for giving us this virtuous woman as a mother.

Janice P. Wright

# I Never Wrote a Poem for My Dad

I never wrote a poem for my Dad. I wrote him plenty of notes though, especially when I was young. I was afraid to ask him in person, that's kind of sad.

Notes like: Dear Daddy, please leave us some lunch money or Hi Daddy, don't forget to leave us bus fair, (sometimes we had to walk to school, you think he cared?)

Hi Daddy, its payday and I knew you would be at 'the Bar' awhile. I couldn't stay up any longer, my report card is on the table (smile).

I wrote him notes that ended with I love you because I just wanted to keep the peace and maybe tonight we could get some sleep.

True to his zodiac sign, Gemini the twin, we never knew what kind of mood he would be in. Nope. I never wrote him a poem.

My Dad would not have understood the expression of emotions and hurt a poem brings about. I should have written a poem about how we walked the streets with no place to go, when he purposely locked us out.

A poem about how he broke our hearts when he beat our mother, or how he embarrassed and disrespected us, would have only made him more furious.

Do you think he would have appreciated all these feelings being communicated? When he was angry, he behaved like a man possessed by the devil, that's an understatement, he behaved like the devil himself. My father was mentally disturbed and needed help. So no, I never wrote a poem for him.

My Dad did not have a sense of humor, he could not take a joke.

He would not have found it amusing, the way we laughed at him when he was drunk and marked the way he spoke. Let the truth be told, he used to say, there were two things he hated, a liar and a theft and he was both. My Dad was a user, an abuser of alcohol, people, and dope.

Even in his drunken stupor, he stole people hearts. "Poor, poor Peter," they would say. But, didn't they know that Peter was poor because he wanted it that way. He refused to be rich, he refused to be anything, anybody wanted him to be. They didn't know him and he didn't know himself. His name wasn't Peter either!

I never wrote a poem to my Dad, because the truth hurts. If I had written a poem for my Dad, I would have commented on his free attitude, his free to neglect his responsibilities attitude. I would have expounded on his don't give a damn about anybody, not even himself attitude. I would have elaborated on love and his lack of showing and expressing it.

Nope, I never wrote a poem for, to or about my Dad!

THEY CAME SO NATURALLY

# Funny Valentine

It was just a dream but I remember it as clear as day. There was Grandma, Granddaddy, and their guests. As I recall, the guests were other relatives that had passed away. Grandma was setting the table. It was a table, fit for a king. I could see that she was as busy as a bee. I stood on the outside, listening to her sing.

She called out to granddaddy, "Frank, how are you coming with the room?" "Hurry, he is on his way, I am so excited, I hope he gets here soon." That's when she noticed me, on the outside looking in. She motioned for me to come join them. But the house did not have any stairs. I couldn't find the stairs to the house, I looked everywhere. I just stood on outside looking in, while grandma stood on the inside looking out. There was so much joy and excitement. I noticed that more guests had arrived. What a party this was going to be.
 I did not want it to start without me.

The very next day, we got the call. Maybe it was the tone of her voice or maybe it was the pause. I knew what she was calling to say, even if she had said nothing at all. I heard it in her voice even before she said his name. I had that funny feeling in my guts, it's always the same.

I looked in my mother eyes, her facial expressions were that of shock and surprise. When did he die? She asked. Sometime early this morning was my aunt's replied. They found him body outside. The doctor said he died from pneumonia. Sorry to give you this kind of news on the phone. I am glad you are not home alone.

Snow, ice and bitter winds, February, is one of the coldest months of year. The death of a loved one is something you don't want to hear. The ground was hard and cold when he was buried. She lost her friend, someone she loved in February.

I never thought of them being friends or lovers. To me, Mommies and Daddies were like sisters and brothers. They never divorced, just separated, far, far away from each other.

I suspect that is why they invented Valentine's Day, to bring some warmth to the month in some kind a way. The roses, flowers, and "I love you" looked beautiful on the heart shaped gravestone. "My funny Valentine, the day he died was the day he was born."

Well, I guess now he is sitting at the table with his mother, father and all the other relatives. Sis must be some kind of happy. I am glad he made it home, considering how he lived.

Janice P. Wright

# FEELIN IT"

*So many times, I think of you, and try so hard not to be blue*
*I remember the way you walked, the way you talked*
*I dream about you and it seem so real, like the tears in my eyes that I now feel*
*But, when I awaken you are not here. Oh, how I miss you, my Love, my Dear*
*I know that you have gone to a better place, but in my mind, I can still see your face*
*I was so blessed to have had you, even if it was for just a little while*
*You made me so very happy. Oh, how I miss your smile*
*I loved you so much, only my heart could tell*
*If wishing would bring you back, I would live at the wishing well*
*Your memories are like a sweet fragrance that fills the air*
*My sorrows are so heavy, often hard to bear*
*Continuing sometimes is so hard to do*
*Yet, I must go on living without you*
*Your memories are all I have to go by*
*So, I will embrace them until the day I die*
*The day will come, when we will reunite*
*So, until then, I'll dream of you, again tonite…*

*In memory of: my son, Tony, (2005), my mother, Nanny, (2003) my father, Ted, (2002), my grandfather, Frank, (2000), and my grandmother, Alberta, (1978)*

# How Can I Sing in a Strange Land

**How Can I sing In a Strange Land?**
With no place to call my own
and no place to call home

I roam,

I roam the country roads of the Deep South
The home of the brave, the slaves, and my ancestor's graves

I roam

I roam the city streets of the north,
Where my feet danced to the rhythm of the beat of the ghetto

Africa?  America?
African American
This land is my land

Janice P. Wright

This land is your land
From Chinatown, to Germantown
To Little Italy, to New Mexico
To Haiti?
Oh Hell No!
You got to go,

Back, back across the ocean waves
Where the captives plunged
to their watery graves

Sail across the Seven Seas
Until you reach the Garden of Eden
It's there in the Motherland
The creation of the first woman and man

It's there you'll hear the Father's voice
saying
Dance! Dance!
Rejoice! Rejoice!
There is no place like home!
There is no place like home!

THEY CAME SO NATURALLY

# OVERCOME

We shall **overcome,**

Yes, we shall

When we overcome self-hatred

Hatred within our own race

Look at it staring us in the face

Killing one another, like Cain,

We kill our own brothers

**OVERCOME**

Are we so confused?

Could it be, because

we don't know what name to use?

Are we, Colored, Negro, Black,

African American. Bi-racial or just Racial?

Red bone, high yellow, brown skin

What's up Black?

Janice P. Wright

That's my Dogg, my Nigga…

Now, I really can't get with that

**OVERCOME**

We shall overcome

When we overcome ignorance,

Like Ebonics

They took prayer out of school

What's next Phonics?

Oh, Mary McCloud Bethune,

Don't you weep

All of us are not asleep

**OVERCOME!**

THEY CAME SO NATURALLY

# LET HE WHO IS WITHOUT, CAST THE FIRST STONE

Throw the stone, I dare you
You talk about them, they talk about you
You don't trust them, they don't trust you
You call them names, they call you names
Throw the stone, go ahead
Stop playing, no more faking it, let's be real
The truth of the matter is…
You are just as fake as they are
Throw it!
 Yeah, you joke and give hidden messages
They aren't joking, although, their messages
are hidden in unspoken words
Words that you don't understand
Why don't they just say what's on their minds?
Why don't you just say what's on your mind?
Bigotry, Racism, Chauvinism, Dogmatism, and
Sexism,
 ALL spells Prejudice
Yeah, putting down that stone
Uh, Huh… I knew it
STOP HATING!
LET'S LOVE!

Janice P. Wright

# We Came…We Saw… We Conquered!

We came…

Seeking the education that was denied our fore parents

Seeking the Freedom of Knowledge, to speak, to teach, to reach

No longer the same, no longer the mis-educated Negro because… We came

We saw…

The struggles of racism, the injustice, the indignity, the dehumanizing of a people,

Lost in a hurricane, left alone in the Superdome

We saw the wars, in the middle-east and on our streets,

Homicides or Genocides?

Don't mean to be political, just being analytical

We conquered…

Not just because but for a Cause

Psychology and Theology, deep in our souls, Messing with our minds

Yes! We were blind, but now we see,

That is it Necessary Beyond Any and All Means

To Conquer Our Quest

To Conquer Our Dreams!

We came …

    We Saw….

        We Conquered!

# I Hear Tales

I know your secrets
The things you don't tell
I know them well
Housing all that vital information
Covering it up with all these beautiful gardens
Farm land now, but once a Plantation!

I know your secrets,
I know them well
The souls you brought were not for sell
Covering up the roots of generations
Burying them in the ground, dividing a nation

Hang low old tree, tell us your story
What did you see, what strange fruit
did you have growing?

Nothing could be finder than to be in Carolina
But I heard it through the grape vine that
everything wasn't so fine
Cry out old ancestors! Buried in the ground
The truth is in our roots, dig them up
so, our offspring will no longer be bound
Cry out, so our children are ignorant no more!

No longer defenseless against society
No more secrets behind closed doors
Tell the tales, that will set them free
His story, Her story, our stories
They rewrote them and took away the glory.
Only the truth will set them free
Tell them the tale of your struggles, your victories

I know your secrets,
I know them well
You thought you could incarcerated them
put them away in cells
But secrets make great hear tales

I hear tales of blood sweat and
tears in the cotton fields
hidden secrets from over the years
Tales of Churches, homes, and properties
mysteriously burned by wild fires
carried away by the wind,
incinerated dreams, and desires

Oh yeah, I know your secrets
I know them well!
Although you want to keep it on the down low,
The truth just won't let go
of secrets that must be told
To heal a people, restore and make them whole.

# My Genesis

In the beginning God created the Heavens and the Earth

For He is the beginning, the Creator, the Alpha,

The Heavens are His dwelling places

The earth His footstool

Now the Earth was without shape or form, just a waste

The Earth was dark and deep was the darkness

Like the earth, I was used as a footstool, stepped on by mankind

My life was without shape or form, with no purpose, just a waste

I lived in darkness and could not find any light,

Great was that darkness.

The waters were deep upon the surface of the earth

As much as the water, covered the earth,

Deep in my soul were the tears of my sorrows

Then God, The Creator, looked upon my mass

God, my Deliver, took a looked at my dark situation

And said, "Let there be light," and the Light came forth

I open my heart and in came the Light

God, My Creator, saw the Light and said, "It is good"

Then God, My Deliver, looked at me and said,

This is my beloved daughter, in whom I am well pleased

Now, let your light shine for Me.

## IN TOUCH

I wanted to get in contact with myself

For I felt as if was slipping

and needed some help

Meditate. Breathe in. Breathe out

Silence was all that came about

Maybe, I should communicate my feeling

by sending myself a letter

No, I needed quick results,

an email would be better,

Perhaps I should call myself

on my cell phone.

Hello self, are you alone?

Maybe, I should take a trip on boat or a ship

Running away, no, that is not the solution

Janice P. Wright

I must face myself and come to

some kind of conclusion

That's when I realized, that I am not alone

Where is my faith, surely that can't be gone?

When I feel like I am sinking, of myself,
I should not be thinking

I need Divine help to see me through

I know what I must do

There is only one who can guide

Only one who is always on my side

So, I whispered a little prayer

God heard me, and that when I notice that he
was right there all the time

Then I breathe in..., breathe out...

Hallelujah! was all I could shout

THEY CAME SO NATURALLY

# THA'S MY POEM

It's not my poem but it is my poem
Even though it wasn't written by me,
It sure was written for and about me
It's my poem because it speaks of…
My struggles, my people and it tell my stories
For real, I could have written tha poem
It's my poem, you know what I mean?
Like when someone says, "Tha's my song,"
or
"Tha's my jam."
Tha's my poem!
It speaks to my soul.
It touches my heart and blows it my mind
Yeah, it's my poem alright.
Girl, how did you get in my head like that?
Got to give you your props
Thank you, Maya, and Nikki G.
for writing my poems for me.

Janice P. Wright

# ME & NIKKI G

I Love Me Some Nikki G

She is so real, so like that, and that's a fact

She is not uncomfortable in her skin

I love me some Nikki G, I wish she was my friend

I imagine the conversations we would have

Girl, you are out of your mind,

Ok, ok, and that's fine

For real, for real, that's how you feel?

No, you did not say that to them

Girl, they got you on film

You wouldn't believe what just happened?

Just thinking of what Nikki G. would say to me

I laugh at myself (LOL)

I just love myself some Nikki G!

She writes about wars, she battles with politics

# THEY CAME SO NATURALLY

She teaches the unrefined,
she messes with people's minds

With her spoken word, she knocks down giants and
she ain't that big!

I saw her one time at a poetry gig

She made those high fluting folks feel so small

I am just sayin, that's all,

They thought they were going to hear another
"namby-pamby" poet

But she was so strong in her words,

When she was finished, opened mouths,
no claps, or shouts,

Boom, mike down, Nikki G, was out!

She left them with something to think about

I was like "No, she didn't, that's my girl!"

To me, she is the best poet in the world.

I love myself some Nikki G!

Janice P. Wright

# MY MAN

**My Man**

Strides with every step he takes,

He runs like a gazelle, he is swift

He walks on water

**My Man**

Carries the weight of the world on his broad shoulders

Never slumping, never bending, never wavering,

He is a strong tower for me to lean on

**My Man**

Chest is a mountain on which I climb

to listen to beat of hot lava as it boils,

rising to top, it warms my whole being

**My Man**

Arms are sculptured boulders,

When he holds me, I succumbed to his gentleness

and I am comforted as he rocks me in his arms

**My Man**

Hands are powerful, legal weapons,

But, when he touches me with those hands

Caress and massage my body, I pass out,

as he gently lay me down to sleep

**My Man,**

Voice roars through the air like thunder,

His laugher is riveting

Only I can understand his lingo

His slang is our thang, our song

He is my poetry man

**My Man**

Eyes are big, brown, and beautiful

They have seen a lot…

A lot of hatred, a lot of envy,

a lot suffering and a lot of pain

**My Man**

When I look into my Man's eyes,

I see nothing but trust and respect,

Nothing but hope, and admiration

And when he looks into mine,

He sees nothing but Love

**My Man,**

hum, um, um **My Man**….

Janice P. Wright

# SOMETIMES

Sometimes, I don't wanna be obligate
Sometime, I don't wanna be tied down
Sometimes, I just wanna be free, free to be me
Free to worship
Free to Sing my song, in or out of tune
Free to dance my dance, in and out of step
Free, free, free to be me
Sometimes, I cry, why?
Because I am sad, I am hurt or mad,
But sometime, I cry because I am happy
Thankful! So grateful!
Sometimes, I wanna just pray, aloud, or softly,
just moan and groan
Sometimes, I pray in the unknown tongues
Sometimes, I wanna to love, be loved,
and do lovely things and sometimes I don't
I don't wanna fake it, don't wanna smile
Don't wanna cloth myself in unnecessary thing
Sometimes, I just want to be Free,
Hiding nothing, just letting it all hang out
Free, free, free to me

# DEAF-CEPTION

If I don't ask no questions, then don't tell me no lies

Because if I only knew the truth, I think I would die

No, don't tell me the truth

No, don't you dare

Only whisper in my ears, the things I want to hear

Shh... Silence is the best

No, no, I don't want to know the rest

Let bygones, be bygones and so longs, be so long

Allow me to create my own picture of how I want things to be,

God loves the truth, so let the truth be between you and He

As for me, whisper in my ears the things I want to hear

Janice P. Wright

# THEY CAME SO NATURALLY

No burning

No smells

No breakage

Lined up like peas in a pod

Naturally curly

They grew

They locked

Some thought they looked odd

Water proof

Weather proof

Wear proof

Wild, hanging loose, and free

Growing

Longer

Stronger

They came so naturally

    Maturity

        Spirituality

           Serenity

My Crown and Glory

    Free to be me

        Beautiful Locs

           Came So Naturally

Janice P. Wright

# Grindin' in the Name of the Lord

He went about his morning routine, he did it faithfully every day. He pumped himself up, like he was getting ready for the big game. He hit the box, hit the floor, and began to exercise, doing one hundred sit ups and pushups. Next, he prayed to God, and then he read his Good New Bible. After that... whatever.

As he was pulling up his pants, he began to recite Ephesians 6: 13-17. He knew these verses by heart. He learned them at the Christian school, his mother made him attend.

Verse 13 - Wherefore take unto you the whole armor of God that ye may be able to withstand in the evil day and having done all to stand. He stood up straight, struck out his chest, held in his stomach and gritted on his self as he looked in the mirror. He took pride in his body, with a smirked on his face, he said "Yea, nobody better mess with me on these streets." I am a child of God and Satan desire to have me but he can't get me. I am evil, but I am saved by grace. I am a sinner, but I am saved by grace. Everybody sins, for we are all sinners, but we are saved by grace. Besides, somebody prayed for me and if they didn't, Jesus did. Yea, He pumped himself up like that all the time. People thought he was mentally disturbed because he talked to himself in this manner. He learned to speak to himself and to encourage himself with the "Word." Aint' that what David did, he

asked himself. That's what keeps me from ……
huh, losing it.

Verse 14 - he recited, Stand therefore, having your loins girt about with truth and having on the breastplate of righteousness. Making up a rap beat, he rapped, "Got my vest on my chest." "Check."

Verse 15 - And your feet shod with preparation of the gospel of peace: Looking down at his feet he sang "Tims on my feet, to keep the peace on the streets, I stomped to the beat." "Check."

Verse 16 – Above all, taking the shield of faith, wherewith ye shall be able to quench all the darts of the wicked. He picked up his cellphone to send a text message to his homies, they were like his disciples. For they trusted him, they had faith in him and they were strapped, like Peter with his sword, ready to defend. "Wha up, are you ready for war, are you ready to defend, like Peter with his sword?" "Check."

Verse 17 – Take the helmet of salvation, and the sword of the Spirit, which is the word of God. "Cap on straight, looking good, niggas gonna be hating." "Check."

"Now," he told himself, "Get ready for the Word of God." He flipped through the pages of the Bible. "David, he thought, was like that, plenty of women, lots of moolah, nice cribs, chariots made of gold, and an army of outlaws, (his crew). "Damnnn, he was bad." His stuff was tight. He shonuff was a man after the heart of God. Let's see what, Psalms 31 has to say." "I come to your Lord, for protection."

Deep, he thought. He read on, "never let me be defeated." "You are a righteous God: save me Lord I pray! He finished reading the word, he began to think about his own enemies, suddenly his mood changed. He became solemn as he kneeled down and began to pray. He called God, "My Man," not Father, not Jesus the Christ but "My Man" He would tell his boys, "My Man" always got my back. When I pray to "My Man," he listens up. He closed his eyes and began his prayer. "What's up *My Man*, it's Ton, Ski Bone, but you know that. Just want to give you your props and ask for protection again da day. Thanks for all you have done, doing, and will do for me. Thanks for keeping me alive and out of jail. Thanks for letting me make my *monay*, rubbing his hands together like he always does when talking about money. "You know what's happenin' on the streets, I need your protection more than ever these days. Feed the babies, clothe the naked and heal the sick. I don't know how you gonna do all that but I know you can. You can multiply bread, fish, and make wine," (huh, he thought with a smile, fish sandwiches & some wine). "Bless my crew, help them to think fast and move faster. Keep us safe from our enemies. Bless our families, especially mine. Let us make a lot of monay, so we can help our families. Bless my Lil Diamond in the rough and her mother. My Man, don't let that girl come down here looking for me again today, I gave her money last week. Forgive me, My Man. I just got off track, just keepin' it real. You know how we go. You are powerful, and mighty in battle. I honor you," ending his prayer by punching himself in the chest, and raising a fist up to God. "Amen."

Now, He was ready for his day…

It is cold and raining outside.  The streets are wet.

Don't matter, he thought, the streets are always cold, cold like death.

The streets are always cold, cold like death…

The streets are always cold, cold like death…

## MORE ABOUT THE AUTHOR

***Janice P. Wright*** is the eldest daughter of the late Mr. Theodore, Sr. and Mrs. Eartha Prather of Aiken, South Carolina and Philadelphia, PA. She is the granddaughter of the late Rev. George, Jr. and Mrs. Mable Burckhalter and Deacon Frank and Alberta Prather of Aiken, SC.

Janice is a wife, mother and grandmother. She is married to Thomas Wright her husband of 33 years. Janice and Thomas worshipped at Life Source International Church in White Marsh, Maryland. Currently, they reside in Aiken, South Carolina.

Janice attended the Baltimore School of the Bible and is a graduate of the Central Christian University, where she earned a degree in biblical studies. In 2014, she was ordained as a Minister of God at Life Source International Church.

Minister Wright is a Mentor, Spiritual Leader, and Biblical Educator for the Debutantes in Christ, (DEBS–IN-CHRIST) a ministry for young ladies. She loves being involved in this ministry because it exposes young ladies to etiquette and culture, allowing them to grow into "Godly Women" fulfilling God's purpose for their lives.

She holds a Bachelor Degree in Healthcare Administration. Janice has over 30 years of experience in health care. She has combined administrative expertise with experiences in leadership development, professional/adult education, and organizational development. She is currently employed with the Federal Government, the Department of Veteran Affairs.

Janice's favorite prayer is the Lord's Prayer. She loves to hear it spoken, sung or hummed. Her deepest ministry desire is that God's Will be done in her life and in the lives of the children of God on earth as it is in Heaven. Amen.

www.ingramcontent.com/pod-product-compliance
Lightning Source LLC
Chambersburg PA
CBHW042053290426
44110CB00006B/171